SPACE SYSTEMS: PATTERNS AND CYCLES

# MOON

Becky Noelle

LIGHTBOX
openlightbox.com

## LIGHTBOX

Go to
**www.openlightbox.com**
and enter this book's
unique code.

**ACCESS CODE**

**LBXK4525**

Lightbox is an all-inclusive digital solution for the teaching and learning of curriculum topics in an original, groundbreaking way. Lightbox is based on National Curriculum Standards.

**OPTIMIZED FOR**

- ✓ TABLETS
- ✓ WHITEBOARDS
- ✓ COMPUTERS
- ✓ AND MUCH MORE!

## STANDARD FEATURES OF LIGHTBOX

**AUDIO** High-quality narration using text-to-speech system

**VIDEOS** Embedded high-definition video clips

**ACTIVITIES** Printable PDFs that can be emailed and graded

**WEBLINKS** Curated links to external, child-safe resources

**SLIDESHOWS** Pictorial overviews of key concepts

**INTERACTIVE MAPS** Interactive maps and aerial satellite imagery

**QUIZZES** Ten multiple choice questions that are automatically graded and emailed for teacher assessment

**KEY WORDS** Matching key concepts to their definitions

**VIDEOS**

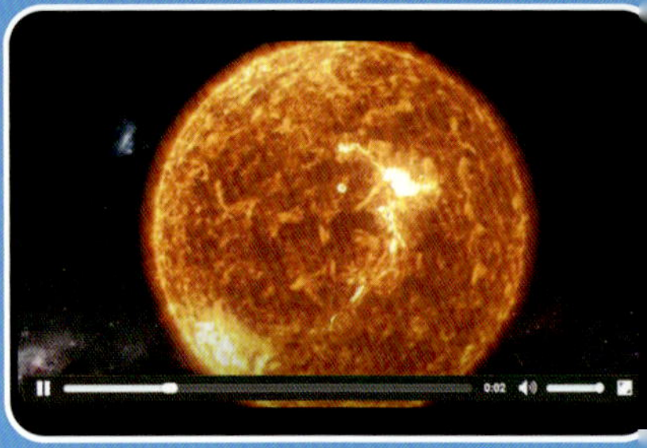

**WEBLINKS**

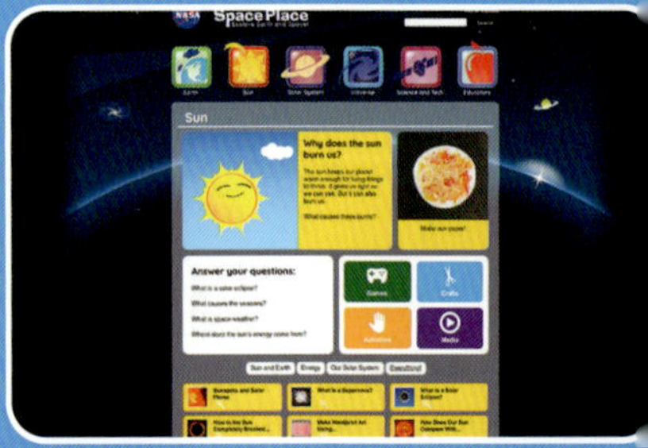


**SLIDESHOWS**

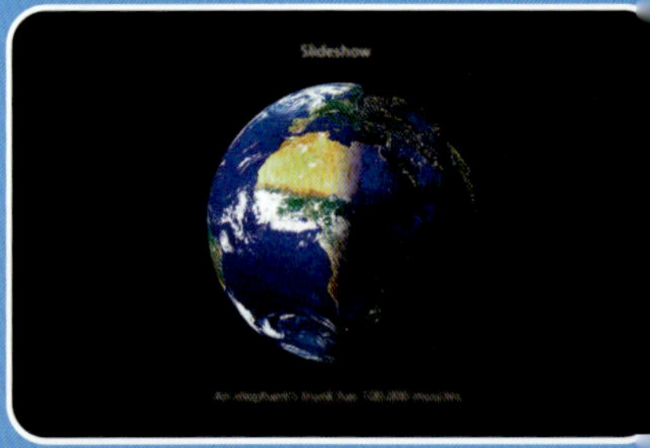


**QUIZZES**

SPACE SYSTEMS:
PATTERNS AND CYCLES

# MOON

## Contents

**The Moon** is our closest neighbor. We see it shining in the night sky.

Did you know that the Moon is **slowly moving away** from Earth? Each year, it moves about 1.5 inches away.

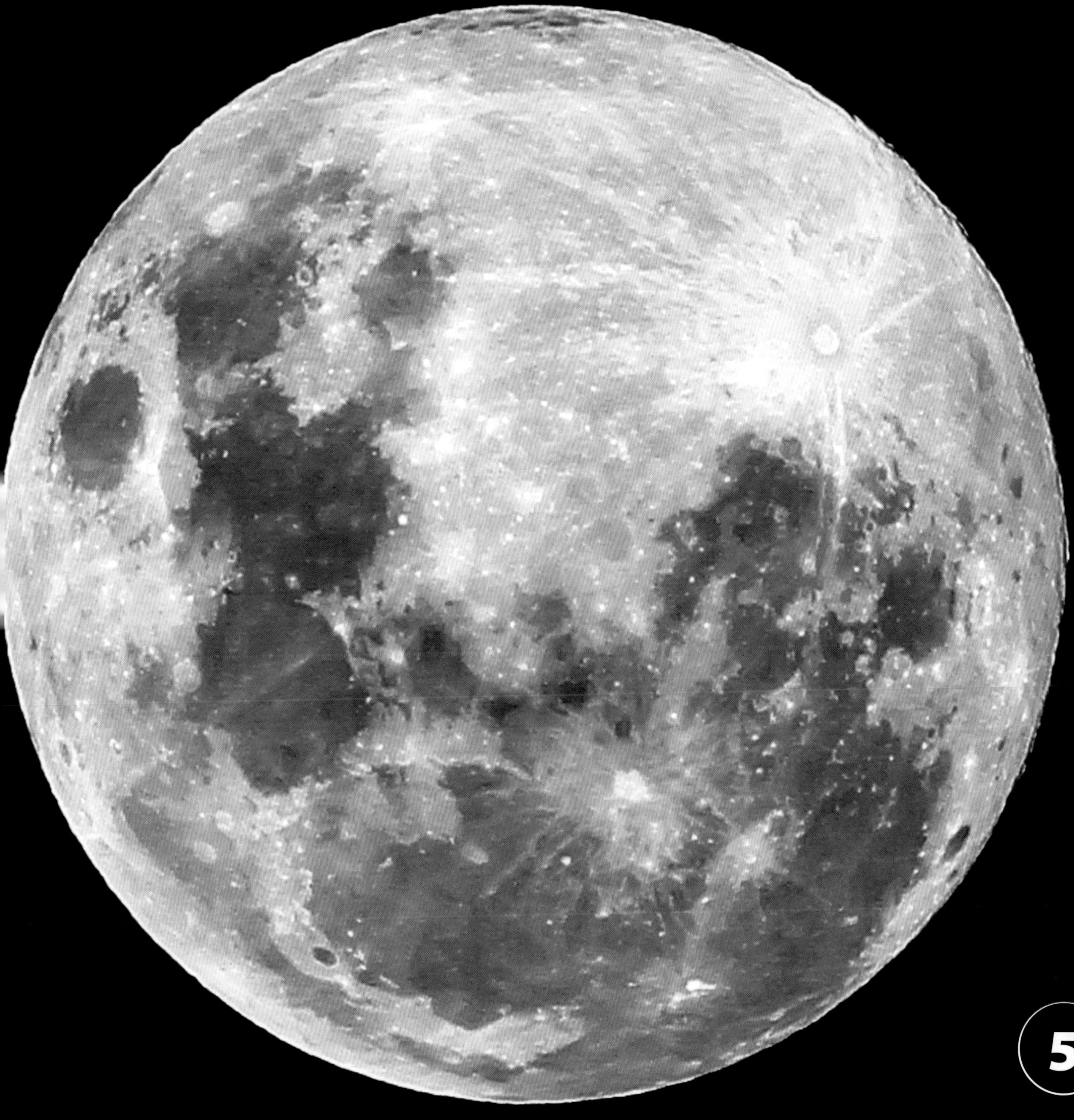

The Moon **orbits** Earth. This means it travels around our planet.

It takes **27 days** for the Moon to orbit Earth.

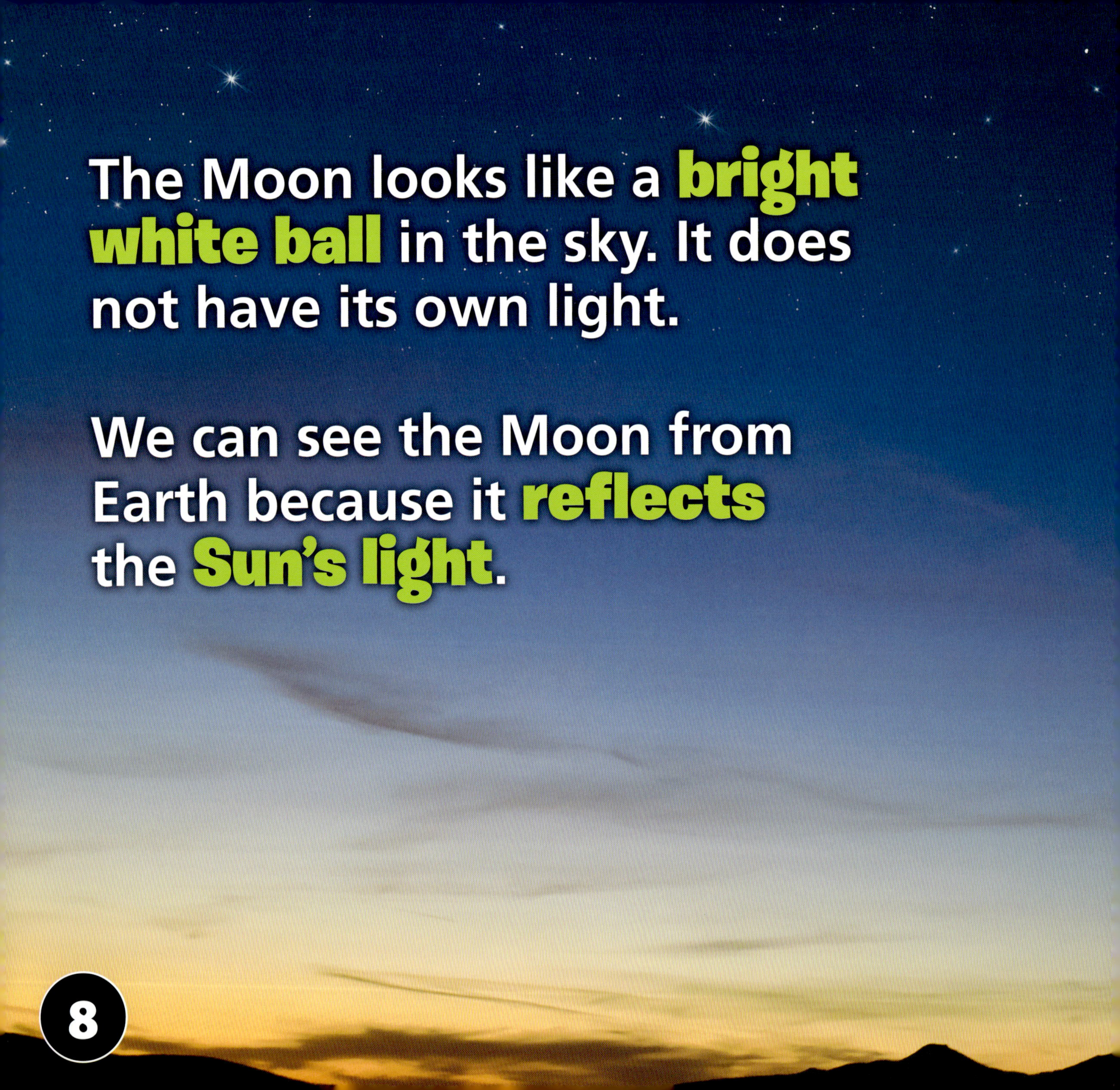

The Moon looks like a **bright white ball** in the sky. It does not have its own light.

We can see the Moon from Earth because it **reflects** the **Sun's light**.

It takes **1.3 seconds** for **light** to travel from the **Moon** to Earth.

The Moon stops Earth from wobbling. That makes the **climate** on Earth milder.

Without the Moon, Earth's **seasons** might be very different.

The Moon **spins** once every time it orbits Earth.

We only ever see **one side** of the Moon.

You can see the Moon at **night** when the Sun shines on it.

The Moon **appears** to move from **east** to **west** across the night sky.

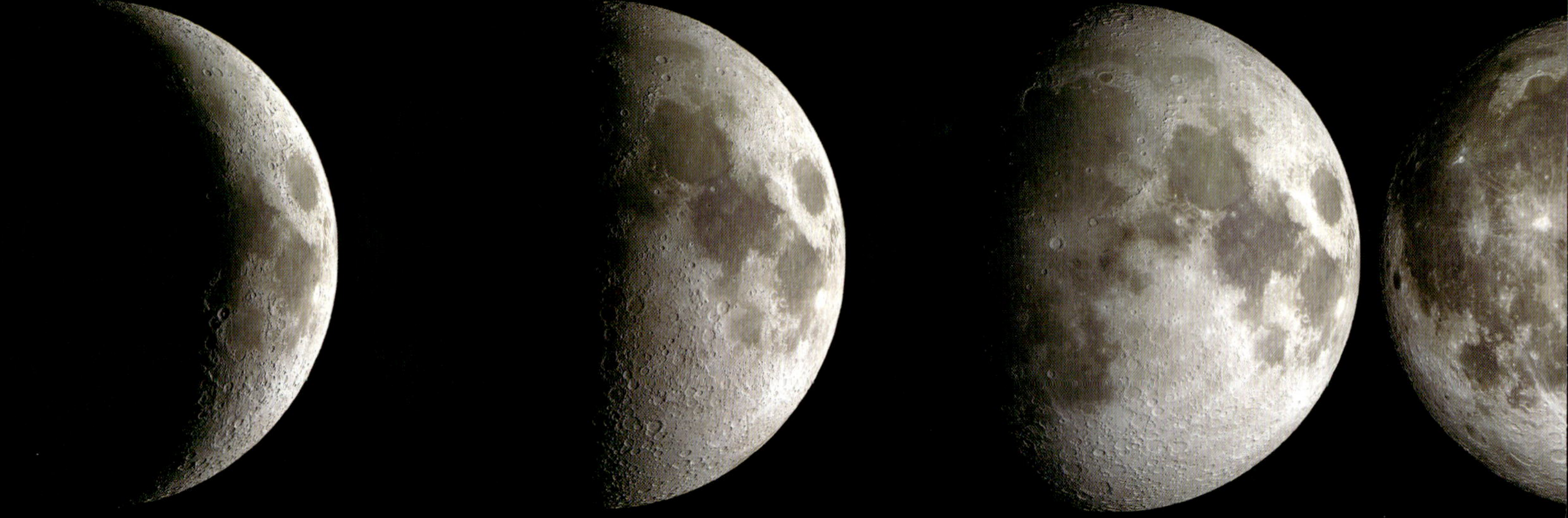

**Moon phases** happen when different parts of the Moon are lit by the Sun.

The four main Moon phases are **New Moon**, **First Quarter**, **Full Moon**, and **Last Quarter**.

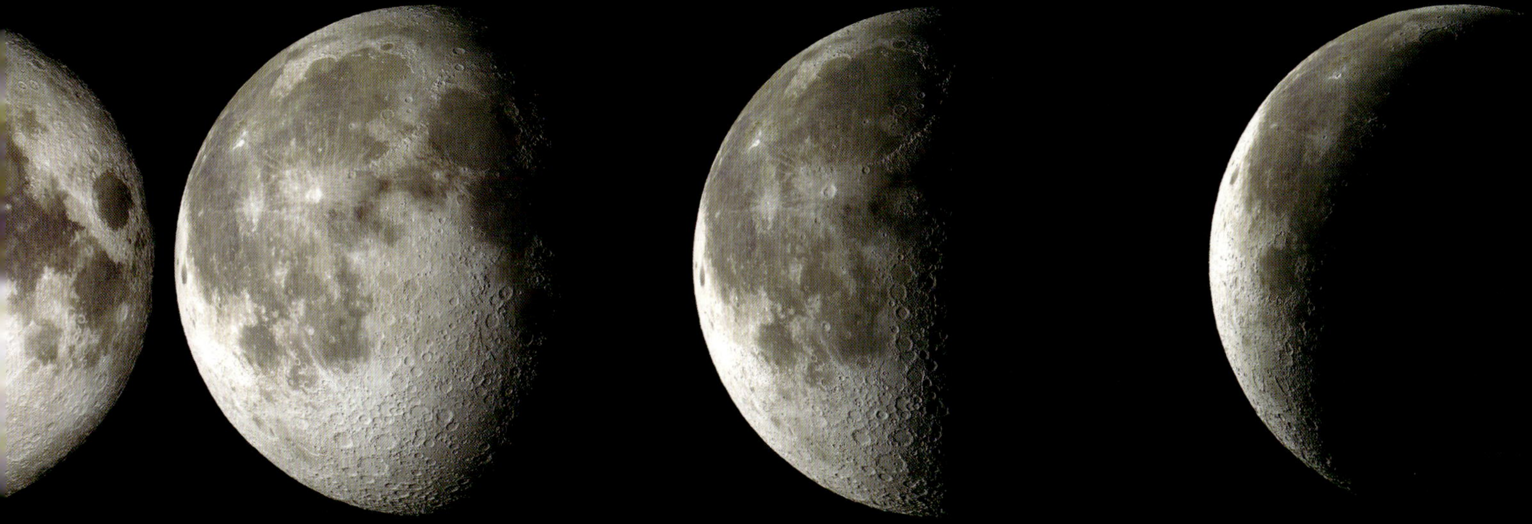

The Moon appears **brightest** at Full Moon.

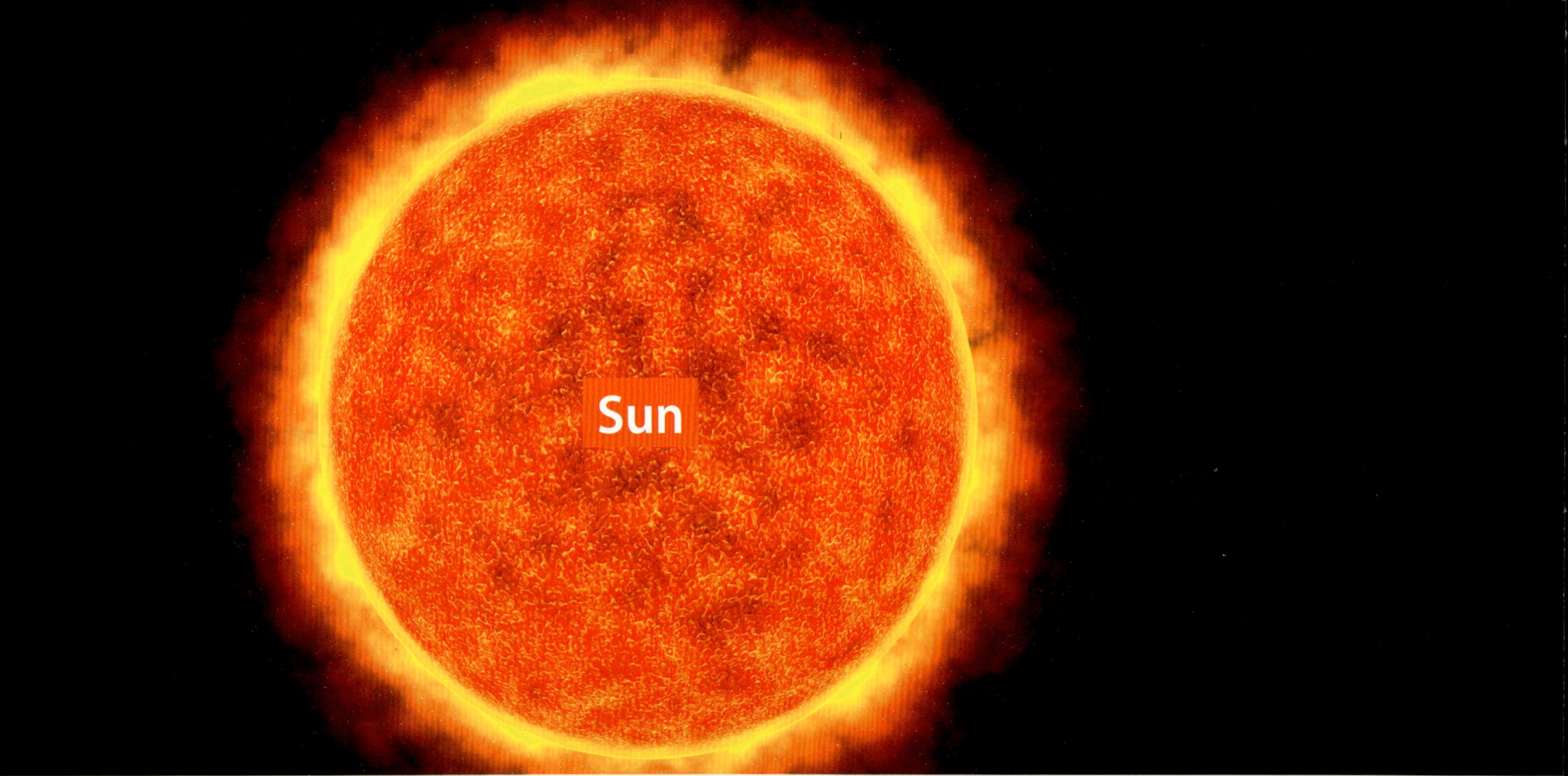

The Moon is between Earth and the Sun. It is a **New Moon**.

The Sun lights up half the Moon. It is a **Quarter Moon**.

Moon

Earth

Earth is between the Moon and the Sun. It is a **Full Moon**.

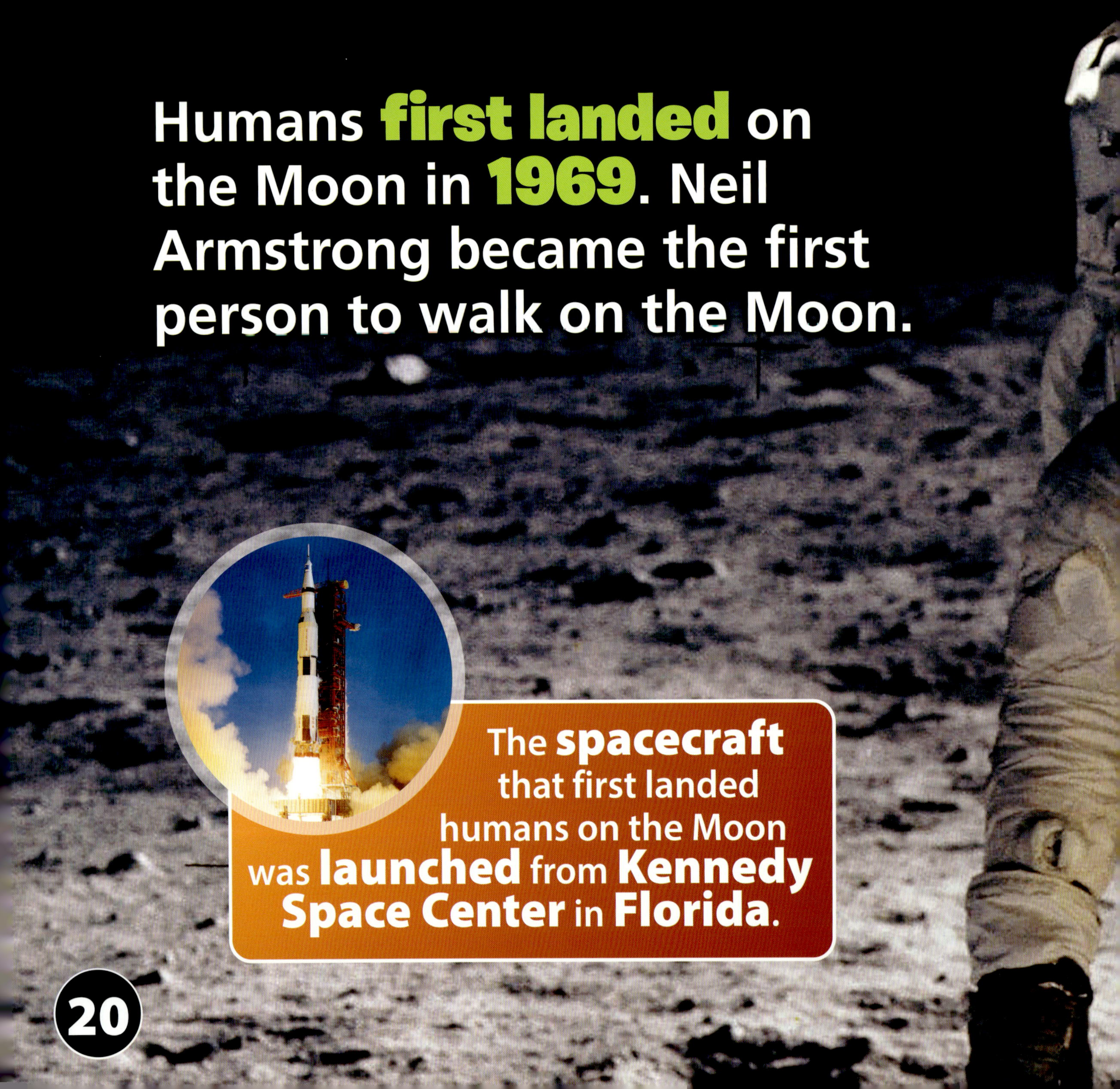

Humans **first landed** on the Moon in **1969**. Neil Armstrong became the first person to walk on the Moon.

The **spacecraft** that first landed humans on the Moon was **launched** from **Kennedy Space Center** in **Florida**.

# Activity: Moon Phases

How does the Moon change? When does each Moon phase happen? You can find out by watching the Moon. Remember, sometimes you may not be able to see the Moon at all.

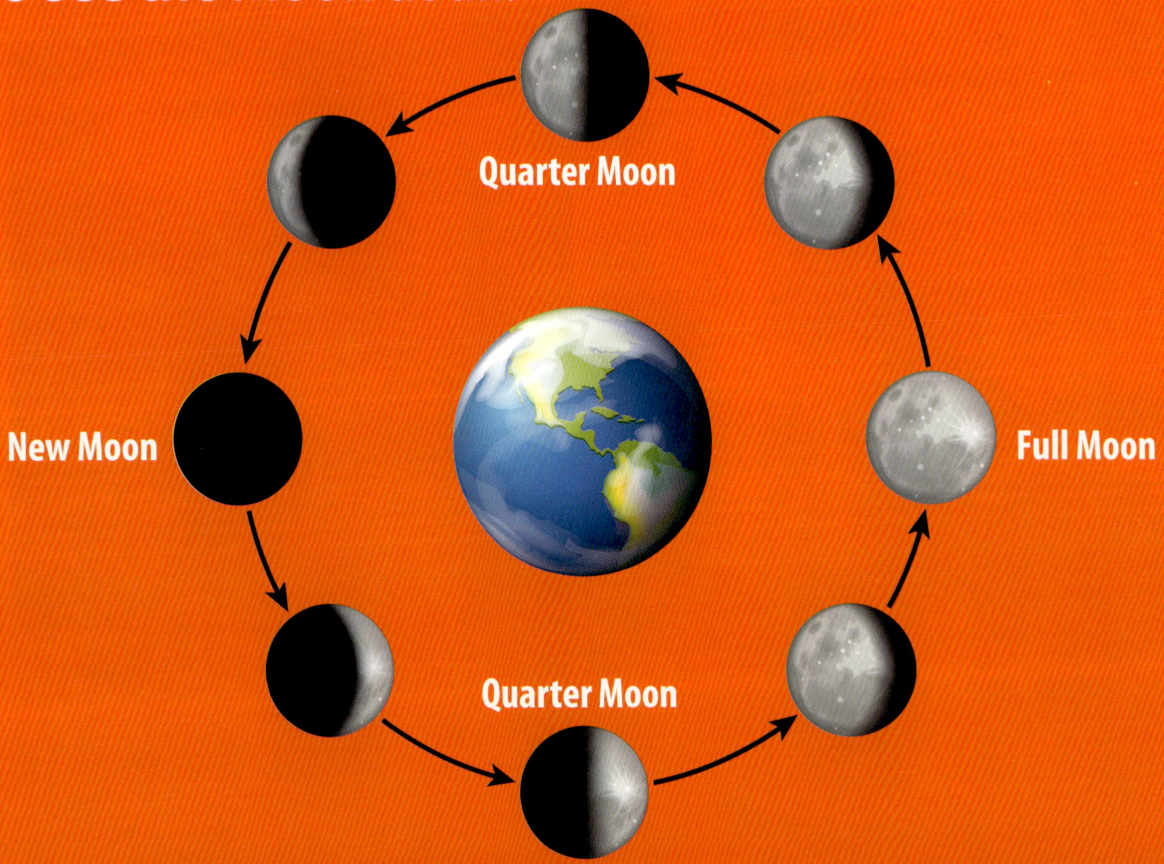

## Steps

1. Put up a calendar.
2. On the first day of a month, observe the Moon and draw its shape in that day's box on your calendar.
3. Repeat Step 2 every day for a month.
4. Match each drawing to its Moon phase. Is it a New Moon, Quarter Moon, or Full Moon?

What did you notice? How did the shape of the Moon change during the month?

# KEY WORDS

Research has shown that as much as 65 percent of all written material published in English is made up of 300 words. These 300 words cannot be taught using pictures or learned by sounding them out. They must be recognized by sight. This book contains 68 common sight words to help young readers improve their reading fluency and comprehension. This book also teaches young readers several important content words, such as proper nouns. These words are paired with pictures to aid in learning and improve understanding.

| Page | Sight Words First Appearance |
|---|---|
| 4 | about, away, did, each, Earth, from, in, is, it, know, moves, night, our, see, that, the, we, year, you |
| 6 | around, means, this |
| 7 | days, for, takes, to |
| 8 | a, because, can, does, have, its, light, like, looks, not, own, white |
| 9 | seconds |
| 10 | makes, on, stops |
| 11 | be, different, might, very, without |
| 12 | every, once, time |
| 13 | of, one, only, side |
| 14 | at, when |
| 16 | and, are, by, first, four, last, new, parts |
| 18 | between, up |
| 20 | walk, was |

| Page | Content Words First Appearance |
|---|---|
| 4 | inches, Moon, neighbor, sky |
| 6 | planet |
| 8 | ball, Sun |
| 10 | climate |
| 11 | seasons |
| 15 | east, west |
| 16 | First Quarter, Full Moon, Last Quarter, New Moon, phases |
| 20 | Florida, humans, Kennedy Space Center, Neil Armstrong, person, spacecraft |

Published by Smartbook Media Inc.
14 Penn Plaza, 9th Floor New York, NY 10122
Website: www.openlightbox.com



Library of Congress Control Number: 2020936989

ISBN 978-1-5105-5530-3 (hardcover)
ISBN 978-1-5105-5531-0 (multi-user eBook)

Printed in Guangzhou, China
1 2 3 4 5 6 7 8 9 0 24 23 22 21 20

052020
110819

Project Coordinator: Priyanka Das
Designer: Ana María Vidal

Every reasonable effort has been made to trace ownership and to obtain permission to reprint copyright material. The publisher would be pleased to have any errors or omissions brought to its attention so that they may be corrected in subsequent printings.

The publisher acknowledges Getty Images, iStock, and Shutterstock as the primary image suppliers for this title.